Old Thornhill

Durisdeer, Enterkinfoot, Carronbridge
Keir Mill, Penpont, Tynron

David Carroll

Durisdeer village *c.*1910. The population of this tiny and remote village nestling in the shadow of the Lowther Hills is considerably smaller today. Weaving was still an important cottage occupation at the end of the nineteenth century although probably declining by the time this picture was taken. Approximately 100 people made their home in the village at the end of the 19th century. Today the number has shrunk to less than 20. Durisdeer was a much more important village in former times. The Well Path, which starts at the other end of the village, follows the track of a Roman Road, which once formed the main route to Edinburgh. The route was also used by medieval pilgrims travelling on their way to and from the monastery at Whithorn.

The old Roman bridge at Durisdeermill. Joseph Laing Waugh, writing in his book *Thornhill and Its Worthies* (1913), recounts how "...on one occasion the Carlisle and Edinburgh coach [which passed through Thornhill en route, where the horses were changed] was snowed up at Durisdeer Mill(sic). It was a tremendous storm, lasting three days, and all communication between the hamlet and outer world was cut off. The passengers were hospitably entertained, but such an unexpected increase in the little population shortened their supply of provisions, and their completely isolated position occasioned fears of famine. A little serving-maid, on looking into one of the passenger's bedrooms, saw him brushing his teeth. Evidently", continued Waugh, "this was a part of the toilet to which she was unfamiliar, for she ran down the lobby crying 'Oh Mistress, we're dune for noo; the gentlemen are beginning to sharpen their teeth wi' a wee white file.'"

 Durisdeer

The remains of 16th-century Kirkbride, which lie in remote country high above the Enterkin Pass. A recent (2000) booklet celebrating three hundred years of worship at Durisdeer recounts how an early-18th century minister of Kirkbride, the Revd. Peter Rae, made a printing press at his manse where he printed the first known books in the south of Scotland. Ordained Minister of Kirkbride on the 22 April 1703, he was not popular with his parishioners who had not had a minister since 1662, and became involved in a series of disputes. These came to a head in July 1713 when fourteen of his parishioners charged him with being "so taken up with mechanics and worldly business that it takes him off his ministerial office ... and that he causes print obscene ballads in his own house." Rae prosecuted his accusers for libel before the Presbytery. The Synod found that most of the charges were not proven. It came out in evidence that Robert Rae [his son] "had printed several copies of the ballad *Maggy Lauder*, in the absence of his father." By 1715 the printing press had been transferred to Dumfries and was operated by Robert Rae. The parish of Kirkbride was suppressed in 1727 by the Lords Commissioners of Teinds. In 1732 the Revd. Rae was transferred to Kirkconnel.

The beginning of a poem that celebrates Kirkbride by Wanlockhead Poet Robert Reid.

Durisdeer Church *c*.1923. Although the main body of this church was built in 1720, it would be almost another decade before the tower was finished. It stands on the site of an earlier place of worship that was demolished in 1716. The church is distinguished by two famous monuments, the Queensberry Marbles, funeral effigies of the second Duke of Queensberry (d. 1711) and his Duchess (d. 1709), part of the rich Baroque Queensberry Aisle. They were sculpted by John van Nost, in 1713. Durisdeer Church has received its share of visitors over the years, including Queen Elizabeth the Queen Mother, Princess Margaret and Neil Armstrong, the first man on the moon. In the foreground stands one of Durisdeer's War Memorials.

The second, a granite obelisk seen right (for the wider parish of Durisdeer) is situated a short distance to the south of Durisdeer and stands at the side of the A702. Careful perusal of the respective lists of names inscribed on the two memorials reveals a slight variation. The ranks of those who fell are omitted from the monument here.

     Durisdeer

Enterkinfoot Mill *c.*1906, with the Enterkin Burn railway viaduct - built in 1850 - in the background. The mill, pictured here with the Enterkin Burn tumbling down by its side, might still have been working when this photograph was taken. It was replaced - in the early years of the 20th century - by a larger meal mill on the opposite side of what is now the A76 trunk road. Local artist James Paterson (1854-1932), is believed to have photographed this mill around the beginning of the 20th century, and to have included it in one of his landscapes. After studying at the Glasgow School of Art and in Paris, Paterson married Eliza Ferguson and settled in the Dumfries & Galloway village of Moniave. He spent over 22 years working in the area. During this time he formed friendships with the group of artists, including Sir James Guthrie and E.A. Walton, who later became known as "The Glasgow Boys".

Enterkinfoot

This eye-catching retaining wall just north of Enterkinfoot, pictured here *c*.1911, was constructed by German engineers and judged to be the bench mark of its type when it was built. Its function is to keep safe and stable the steep-sided bank supporting the track carrying rail traffic on the stretch of line between Thornhill and Sanquhar.

               Enterkinfoot

A passenger train steaming past Tunnel Cottage, Enterkinfoot, *c*.1913. The tunnel in question is Drumlanrig Tunnel, which is just under 1400 yards in length and travels almost 200 feet below the surface. Together with various cuttings carved out along the section of track from Thornhill northwards, the tunnel would have served as a useful device to shield the occupants of Drumlanrig Castle from seeing the railway in operation once the line opened in 1850. Building the tunnel was a highly labour-intensive business, and local clay-pits were used as a source for the bricks needed in the construction. Waddels Loch, to the west of the tunnel's northern entrance, was named after the project's chief engineer.

Carronbridge *c.*1906. "...this curious little village, perched on the side of a gorge where the Nith cuts its way through the hills beyond Thornhill, has a character all its own", enthused a correspondent in the *Dumfries and Galloway Standard* in November 1961. "Not perhaps so quiet and restful as it once was", he continues, referring to the ever-increasing volume of traffic on the A76, Carronbridge nevertheless preserves "...an atmosphere of warmth and friendliness which more than compensates for its few deficiencies in other directions." Earlier known as Mortonmill, the village is flanked by two castles: Morton to the east and Tibbers to the west. Tibber's Castle was captured by Robert the Bruce and his followers after the Comyn murder, but the victory was short lived and John of Seton was captured when Tibbers fell once more and hanged by Edward at Newcastle on August 4, 1306. Tibbers was not recaptured by Scottish forces until about 1312. Carronbridge can also boast four Roman forts. These, together with circular enclosures and the site of a motte-and-bailey castle, make the village a spot of considerable archaeological interest.

          Carronbridge

Morton Castle, *c*.1922. Lying at the end of an offshoot of the minor road between Durisdeer and Carronbridge, the remains of the castle are partly embraced by Morton Loch, providing a most attractive setting. A castle was first built at Morton in 1307 but dismantled under the terms of the 1357 Treaty of Berwick between England and Scotland. The castle whose remains stand today was re-built in the mid 1400s by the Earls of Morton, whose family were granted the land in 1440. Writing in *Durisdeer and Vicinity*, David Patterson recounts how "...many years ago the interior of the castle was cleared...but nothing of importance was found beyond a cannon ball, with pieces of a spear, and there was some charred wood, as if the building had been destroyed by fire." The castle was indeed captured and burned during James VI's campaign against John, 8th Lord Maxwell in 1588. Ownership of the remains passed back to the Morton family for a while, before being sold in the early 1600s. Parts of it were still habitable until at least 1714, after which it was abandoned and, despite its remote location, used as a quarry until repairs of what little remained were begun in 1890.

Carronbridge Station (*c.*1950) was on the Glasgow, Dumfries and Carlisle section of the Glasgow and South Western Railway. A correspondent, writing in the *Dumfries and Galloway Standard* in October 1850 shortly after the line opened, enthused: "When in the full flush and glory of summer, the scenery from above Sanquhar and on to Closeburn is beautiful exceedingly... In the short space of three hours and a half," he added, "the traveller can now pass betwixt Glasgow and Dumfries and, while hurried rapidly along, view many scenic illustrations of Scotland's acquired wealth and natural beauty." The station at Carronbridge closed on 7 December 1953, and the present journey time on the same route from Dumfries to Glasgow is about 1 hour 50 minutes.

The Caul on Carron Water at Carronbridge *c*.1921. It was constructed in the 19th century to provide power for Carronbridge Sawmill and Morton Meal Mill. The Caul was destroyed during a great storm in the 1950s, but a few of its remains are visible on either side of Carron Water together with scraps of the iron mechanism used for diverting the water.

Carronbridge 1910. It must have caused a considerable stir, when the men of the Scottish Rifles arrived at Carronbridge to camp on the outskirts of the village for a few weeks of manoeuvres and training exercises during the summer of 1910. The extensive camp, seen here with its forest of tents, would undoubtedly have attracted many sightseers from the surrounding area and been considered an important event, but it seems to have gone unreported in the local press of the time. Carronbridge continued to have military links well into the 20th century; an R.A.F. camp and Prisoner-of-War camp were sited nearby during the Second World War.

 Carronbridge

Gatelawbridge, Thornhill, *c*.1913. The explorer, Joseph Thomson, after whom the Thomson's Gazelle was named, grew up here from the age of ten when his father leased the local red sandstone quarries in 1868. From his home here, the stone-cutter Robert Paterson, the original of Sir Walter Scott's *Old Mortality*, set out in 1758 on his forty years' quest around the country repairing and putting up gravestones to Covenanting martyrs. During this time he returned to his wife and family only occasionally, and in one instance stayed away for ten years.

Thornhill, *c.*1913 looking down from the top of New Street to its junction with North Drumlanrig Street. The tower of Morton Parish Church can be glimpsed peeping above the rooftops, with the slopes of Auchenleck Hill rising in the distance. With its mixture of predominantly 19th-century houses and cottages lining either side of the road, the character of New Street remains pleasingly intact today. One major change in its overall appearance, however, occurred in 1970, when the building at the top of the street housing Dr. Grierson's "Museum of Antiquities" was demolished and replaced by the very modern-looking Briery Park residential home for the elderly.

Thornhill Station, *c*.1912, was a station on the Glasgow, Dumfries and Carlisle section of the Glasgow and South Western Railway. The station, which opened in 1850 and closed on 6th December 1965, lay just over one mile east of Thornhill. Its somewhat distant position is said to result from the fact that the Duke and Duchess of Buccleuch at that time did not want railway trains to be visible from Drumlanrig Castle. The former station house is now a private residence. Today, Dumfries and Sanquhar are the stations closest to Thornhill.

Bowling has been a popular activity in Thornhill for almost two hundred years, with the village boasting its own green since at least the early 1830s. This photograph, taken *c.*1925, appears to show a match in progress on what was described by the *Dumfries and Galloway Standard* in 1961 as "one of the finest greens in the South of Scotland." In those days, Thornhill's bowling club comprised something between 40 and 50 members, each of whom paid an annual subscription of 6/- (30p). By the 1990s, according to research compiled by the pupils of Wallace Hall Primary School, the club - situated off East Morton Street - had added carpet bowling and short mat bowling to its winter activities.

Thornhill District Hospital, *c*.1920. The origins of the hospital go back to the last quarter of the 19th century, when an outbreak of scarlet fever at nearby Penpont claimed the lives of more than twenty children in the course of one year. Not surprisingly, local residents pleaded for an Infectious Diseases hospital to be built in the village but it was to be some years before any proposals came to fruition. When plans were eventually finalised, the decision was made to build the new hospital at Thornhill, where it was erected in Townhead Street in 1900. Thornhill Hospital remains in use today (although, thankfully, no longer dedicated to infectious diseases), and there is also a Health Centre on the site, opened in 1978.

South Drumlanrig Street, Thornhill, *c*.1912. This tranquil scene, disturbed only by a few leisurely horse-drawn vehicles, is a far cry from the Thornhill of today, bisected as it is by the busy A76, of which South and North Drumlanrig Street form a part. "Passed through the village of Thornhill built by the Duke of Queensberry", recorded William Wordsworth's sister, Dorothy, in her journal while making her way to Leadhills and Wanlockhead in 1803. "The 'brother-houses' so small that they might have been built to stamp a character of insolent pride on his own huge mansion at Drumlanrigg(sic), which is in full view on the opposite side of the Nith."

Museum House, Thornhill, *c.*1909. This handsome building at the top of New Street was the home of local G.P. Dr. Grierson. Here, from 1872 until his death in 1899, he single-handedly amassed a large collection of diverse items of interest. (Prior to 1872 he had begun this collection at his earlier, smaller home in North Drumlanrig Street). "Every spare minute was devoted to this hobby", recalled Waugh in *Thornhill and Its Worthies*. "Even when diagnosing a case, if his eye caught an old teapot, a rusty sword, or anything of interest from a far-off clime, he allowed his mind to wander with his eye." This building was demolished in 1970, (Briery Park, a 31 bed residential home for older people now stands on the site), and Dr. Grierson's collection - which he left as a gift to Thornhill, together with one thousand pounds for its upkeep - was divided among other museums.

A crowd in holiday mood gathers near the Cross on the day of Thornhill's Cattle Show in 1911. The event proved a great success, as the *Dumfries and Galloway Standard* reported on 20th September. "The eighty-fourth show of Nithsdale Agricultural Society...deserves to rank as one of the most notable in its history...It is seldom that farm work is so well forward in mid-September, and those engaged in rural pursuits were able to attend in larger numbers than usual. The weather too was favourable...the sun came out in the afternoon when the popular events were proceeding and imparted an almost summer-like brilliance to the scene. The show itself not only maintained the high standard of former years, but surpassed it. This was particularly true in the case of Ayrshires, and yesterday's display of the popular and useful breed was pronounced to be the finest held this year in Scotland...The

20   **Thornhill**

Dabton, near Thornhill, *c.*1910. Designed by the London architect William Atkinson and built in 1820, John Gifford, in his *Buildings of Scotland: Dumfries and Galloway* (2002 edn.), describes this "...villa-classical country house" as "...an interesting jigsaw". Fashioned out of pink sandstone ashlar, Dabton was built to accommodate the Chamberlain of the Drumlanrig estate and, symbolically perhaps, from the grounds at the back of the house, Drumlanrig Castle can be seen in the distance peeping through the treetops. Occasionally, the general public is able to admire the house (from the outside, at least,) and to enjoy the grounds, when the gardens are thrown open (times advertised) under Scotland's Gardens Scheme. On such a day when I paid a visit, there was a roaring trade being done in afternoon tea around the stable-block and courtyard.

Templand, near Thornhill, *c.*1909. This early-18th century farmhouse was the home of Walter Welsh, grandfather of Jane Baillie Welsh who married the writer and historian, Thomas Carlyle here in October 1826. J.M. Sloan described the occasion in his book *The Carlyle Country* (1904). "Carlyle and his brother, Dr. John, abode at the inn in Thornhill village... over the Monday night. On the Tuesday morning, the small, private family party assembled at the farm - old Walter Welsh, the grandfather; his unmarried daughter, Jean, Dr. John Carlyle and the officiating minister and the bride and bridegroom. Carlyle wore the traditional white gloves, and never bridegroom more thoroughly merited such hymeneal adornment. So private a wedding was rare in Nithsdale... The young couple... left Templand by the coach the same day." The old farm buildings adjacent to the house and set around a courtyard, have now been converted into six attractive holiday cottages.

Drumlanrig Castle, Thornhill, *c*.1910. Dating from the late-17th century this seat of the Dukes of Buccleuch and Queensberry took more than ten years to complete. Today, the pink sandstone castle and its grounds are a highly popular tourist attraction with nature trails, cycle routes, craft workshops, the Scottish Cycle Museum and a traditional blacksmith's forge among the many diversions available. Dorothy Wordsworth visited Drumlamrig while touring Scotland in 1803 with her brother William and Samuel Taylor Coleridge. "This mansion", she confided to her journal, "is indeed very large, but to us it appeared like a gathering together of little things. The roof is broken into a hundred pieces, cupolas etc., in the shape of casters, conjuror's balls, cups and the like..."

Holmhill, *c.*1905. Situated just to the west of Thornhill, and close to Templand, Holmhill was sometimes visited by Thomas Carlyle, where he stayed with its occupants Dr. Russell and his wife. Waugh recounts in *Thornhill and Its Worthies* how "...when living at Holmhill with the Russells [Carlyle] had a favourite spot in the grounds to which he frequently retired. Here, under a tree, Dr. Russell instructed his 'man', Andrew Hunter, to make a seat...which is still known as Carlyle's Seat. He sat there for hours at a stretch smoking a long churchwarden pipe, unconscious of the excitement his great presence caused, and deaf to all entreaties to go inside and meet the many high-born visitors who called to pay their respects."

The remains of Morton Old Church, Thornhill. There had been a simple, small ecclesiastical building on the site probably since the end of the 12th century, but the gable end pictured here dates from the late-1700s when the church was completely rebuilt (although not increased in size). It fell into disuse, however, during the 1830s, when the congregation outgrew the limited space available. "There it stands, a time worn relic of a bygone age", lamented Waugh in *Thornhill and Its Worthies*, "unheeded, forgotten, the undisturbed domain of spirits of the past...How many voices - long since silenced - have been lifted up in praise within these rough-hewn walls?" It was succeeded by the present, and much larger, Morton Parish Church in 1841.

Morton Parish Church, in East Morton Street, Thornhill, was designed by the Edinburgh-born architect William Burn. Built in 1841 to replace the smaller Morton Old Church, and with sufficient space to accommodate a congregation of 1200 people, the cost of erecting the new church - said to be in the region of three-and-a-half thousand pounds - was met by the Duke of Buccleuch, who was the church's patron and remained in that capacity until 1874, when such support was abolished.

Capenoch House, Thornhill *c.*1910.. The present house, in the Scottish Baronial style, was built on the site of an earlier house of the same name in the mid-1780s. It was substantially added to by David Bryce (1803-1876) in the early 1850s. Capenoch House, sometimes described as a 'time capsule', has been in the Gladstone family since 1850 and John Gladstone wrote about it in *Transactions of the Dumfries and Galloway Natural History Society*, (11th January 1929). "[It] is one of the latest examples in the county of an important house planned and built by local workmen, with local ideas and local methods", he explained. "We have perhaps in Capenoch a clue to how house building would have developed in the South of Scotland had that district remained impervious to English influences."

Looking south along Townhead Street, Thornhill, *c.*1912. Virginhall Church is on the right-hand side of the road at the junction with West Morton Street. Formerly Thornhill United Presbyterian Church and built in the closing years of the 19th century, the building was designed by the Glasgow architect, John B. Wilson (1849-1923). It was described by Gifford, in *Buildings of Scotland: Dumfries and Galloway*, as "Scots late Gothic". It is constructed of red sandstone from the local quarry at Gatelawbridge. The horse-drawn, barrel-laden cart on the near right might be an early-20th century milk float, or the carter may be delivering water from door to door.

Courthill Smithy, Keir Mill, *c*.1912. This roadside building boasts three plaques, erected at intervals over the years, celebrating the great achievement of Kirkpatrick MacMillan who, like his father, worked as a blacksmith here. In 1840, he built the world's first pedal-driven bicycle in this smithy, and travelled on it as far afield as Glasgow taking two days, we are told, over the 70-miles' journey. MacMillan had been inspired by seeing the two-wheeled Hobby Horse, which was pushed along by means of the rider's feet hitting the ground from time to time. After neglecting to patent his invention, it was inevitably reproduced by other people. Commercial manufacture did not begin until well after his death in 1878. His original machine is no longer in existence, but a replica of it can be seen in the Scottish Cycle Museum at Drumlanrig. MacMillan, who worked as a farm labourer before becoming a blacksmith, is buried in the old churchyard at Keir Mill. As the red sandstone plaque - placed on the smithy wall by the 'National Committee on Cycling' to mark the centenary of MacMillan's invention - concludes, "He builded better than he knew."

Keir Mill

Keir Mill *c*.1910. (The eponymous mill, built in 1771, has been converted into a house). The wider parish of Keir can lay claim to another illustrious son besides the inventor of the bicycle, Kirkpatrick MacMillan: Allan Cunningham, poet and all-round man of letters, was born in 1784 in a now demolished cottage near Blackwood House close to the Nith. He wrote a biography of Robert Burns and *Traditional Tales of the English and Scottish Peasantry* but his national reputation, rests on a handful of poems, including *A Wet Sheet and a Flowing Sea* and *The Lovely Lass of Preston Mill*. He came to know Walter Scott, to whom in 1820 he submitted a verse play called *Sir Marmaduke Maxwell* (also published in 1822). Scott pays this poem a compliment in the preface to his *Fortunes of Nigel*.

          Keir Mill

Waterside House, near Keir Mill, *c.*1911. The house was built in the 18th century, and stands in peaceful country at the end of a long tree-lined drive, which leads off the road to the south of Keir Mill. As its name might suggest, this impressive period house with its stone facade lies beside Scaur Water a short distance from where it enters the Nith. The owner of the house in 1836 was one James Hogan, Esq. of Waterside whose grandfather "purchased the property from a family of the name of Orr" according to the *Scottish Statistical Account* of 1834-45. Alexander Orr had acquired the property by marrying Agnes Dalrymple of Waterside in 1725 whose family "had long possessed it".

The manse at Keir Mill which, according to Gifford in his *Buildings of Scotland: Dumfries and Galloway*, was built in 1777 and enlarged greatly in 1828. According to the *Scottish Statistical Account* of 1834-45, "It [now] contains three sitting-rooms and six bedrooms, besides a large sunk story".

          Keir Mill

Keir Mill Upper School *c.*1911. The *Statistical Account* of 1834-45 states that the school house and the house of one of the masters were "built by subscription" but that the heritors "granted a considerable additional and repairs for the Upper Schoolhouse and school." The building has suffered the same fate as countless village schools over the years and is now in private hands.

Although there is a weight limit of 8 tonnes and only one vehicle is allowed on the bridge at a time, this distinctive metal bridge, pictured in its early days *c*.1911, still carries traffic across Scaur Water on the minor road from Keir Mill to Burnhead. One of the Nith's largest tributaries, Scaur Water joins Nithsdale's principal river about a mile south-east of this bridge.

Left: The War Memorial at Keir Mill, *c*.1920. The red sandstone cross stands close to the church, beside the road leading from Keir Mill to Penpont. The shaft of the tall cross bears the inscription: 'To the Glory of God and to the memory of the men of Keir Parish who gave up their lives in the Great War 1914-1918'. Their names are inscribed on the base. Later, the names of those from the parish who fell in the Second World War were added.

Right: Driving along the A702 between Thornhill and Penpont, it is easy to overlook this ancient cross (possibly dating from the 12th century) which stands in a field close to Nith Bridge protected by a circle of iron railings. The origins of this slim sandstone pillar, about ten feet high, are cloaked in mystery. One suggestion is that it might have been put up as a shrine for travellers passing by. A local parish history concludes that "...no accounts can be got of it worthy of being recorded." Not far along the same road, standing in another field just outside Penpont a second - much more recent - intriguing landmark can be seen: the 'pinecone' sculpture created by local Penpont artist Andy Goldsworthy.

Main Street, Penpont, *c.*1909., In *Burns-Lore of Dumfries and Galloway* (1988), James A. Mackay records that when Robert Burns was working as an excise man in the area - *c.*1790 - Penpont parish had less than 1,000 inhabitants, of whom barely a tenth resided in the village itself. Nevertheless, the community was served by seven pubs, and it was outside one of these hostelries that Burns was set upon by smugglers while in the course of his duties.

        Penpont

Main Street, Penpont, looking west, *c*.1911. The village grew into its present shape in the early-19th century, when the amalgamation of small farms into fewer larger ones brought in many people, who had been uprooted in the process, from the outlying hamlets of Burnhead, Brierbush and Townhead. Joseph Laing Waugh, in *Thornhill and Its Worthies*, explains how the village may have originally acquired its name. "From an old manuscript I learn that a wooden bridge was in existence [at the spot where the present Nith Bridge stands] in the fourteenth and fifteenth century. Toll of one penny was exacted at Penpont, hence the name of that village: Pen or penny and pont – Latin for a bridge."

Penpont   37

Cattle grazing on the Glebe, Penpont, in the early 1900s. From the picture it seems possible that the cattle may be what were known as "Scottish Shorthorns", one of the breeds used to improve the Ayrshires during the 19th century. As the oldest recorded breed of cattle in the UK, the Coates's Herd Book began registering Shorthorn cattle in 1822. Shorthorns are typically either red, red and white, white, or roan. The Shorthorn roan colour, when it occurs, is a close mixture of red and white, which is found in no other breed of cattle. During the early part of the twentieth century, Shorthorn/Highland crosses were used extensively to produce high-quality forage-based beef. In Shorthorn history, the names of Bates, Booth and Cruickshank are renowned. Bates and Booth were based in the North of England and developed what are usually referred to as "English Shorthorns." Cruickshank was a Scot who developed the "Scottish Shorthorns". Cruickshank's cattle were thicker, blockier and meatier, and it was their progeny which subsequently evolved into the Beef Shorthorn. Shorthorn genetics are reputed to have been used throughout the globe in the development of over 40 different breeds.

Cairnmill Falls, Scaur Water, Penpont, *c*.1925. Scaur Water, with its wooded and rugged banks, can conjure strong emotions if the author of an old parish history is to be believed. "Call it sentiment if you like", he declares, "but there is no prettier walk to be found than by the banks of our beautiful stream."

Glenmarlin Pool in the course of Scaur Water, Penpont. The clothes worn by the visitors pictured here suggest this photo was taken during the 1930s. Perhaps the hopeful fisherman, fixed intently on his rod, is familiar with a short verse (above) from a local guide book, which is attributed to a literary-minded Penpont apprentice of many years ago. Unfortunately, in the nineteenth century, poaching was apparently a considerable industry on the Scaur and the river is described in the Scottish Statistical Accounts as "a considerable stream, and at one time abounded greatly in trout." Regarding the salmon fishing on the Scour, the writer bitterly comments that "The present state of the law as it refers to the Nith and its tributary streams, is considered by many to be injudicious." He continues "It closes the rivers as early as the 25th of September, when the fish are in excellent order. The angler is then deprived of his recreation, which might with safety be extended for several weeks, and the fish are in fact preserved for those less scrupulous about legal prohibitions."

       Penpont

Main Street, Penpont, looking east, *c.*1903. Nowadays, Thornhill and Dumfries are the nearest main shopping centres for Penpont villagers, but it was a different story in the early 1900s. In those days local residents could not only buy their meat and groceries, but they could also be measured for a new suit or have their shoes made or mended without ever leaving the village.

Itinerant hawkers and pedlars, men who travelled from one village to another selling small household and agricultural wares, or even doing a little seasonal work here and there, were very much a part of the rural landscape during the 19th century. One such person was Johnnie Morgan, pictured here towards the end of his surprisingly long life (given the hardships he must have endured over the years), accompanied by his beloved donkey Tommy and dog Quharrie. Thought to have been born in Kirkconnel, he spent his life wandering the south of Scotland in all weathers, and died in the Poorhouse at Thornhill in 1901, aged 85. Such was the impression he made on those he met, that he became the subject of a poem, which begins:

The Bridge and Shinnel Water, Tynron, *c.1913*. According to *Public Roads and Bridges in Dumfriesshire 1650-1820* by James Robertson (Ed. Gordon S. Robertson, 1993 edn.), an earlier stone bridge was built over Shinnel Water at Tynron Church c.l719. Then, after various repairs had been effected over the intervening years, on 30th April 1782 a "...Mr. Fergusson represented that the Bridge over Water of Shinnel at Tynron Church fell during the late floods...". Because the route was an important one between Galloway and Edinburgh, a new bridge was commissioned "...not exceeding two hundred and thirty pounds sterling." It was satisfactorily completed in 1786.

Dalmakerran, Tynron, cica.1906. During the 19th century it was commonplace for large country houses to be rented out for the summer months while their owners decamped to London or, perhaps, Edinburgh for 'the season'. Whether or not this was the case with Dalmakerran it is hard to judge, but more than once a notice appeared in the *Dumfries and Galloway Standard* announcing that the property was "to be let furnished for the summer months". On one such occasion, in April 1895, the house was described as "of modern construction [with] three public rooms, five bedrooms...cloak and bathroom (hot and cold water)...stabling for six horses...golfing and river fishing in the neighbourhood..." etc. It was also thought important enough to mention that the house was only a "quarter of a mile distant from the Postal and Telegraph Office at Tynron." In the days before instant communications, this may well have proved a vital consideration.

A list of voters of 1868 shows a Mr. Robert Kennedy of Dalmakerran and his son Mr. William Kennedy. These were among the most important propertied men of the area. When the Education (Scotland) Act passed in 1872, local school boards had to be appointed. The first five member board for the area was:

Rev. David Couper, Minister of Tynron
Robert Kennedy, Dalmakerran
Adam Brown, Bennan
Thomas Haining, Laight
James Laurie, Merchant, Tynron Kirk

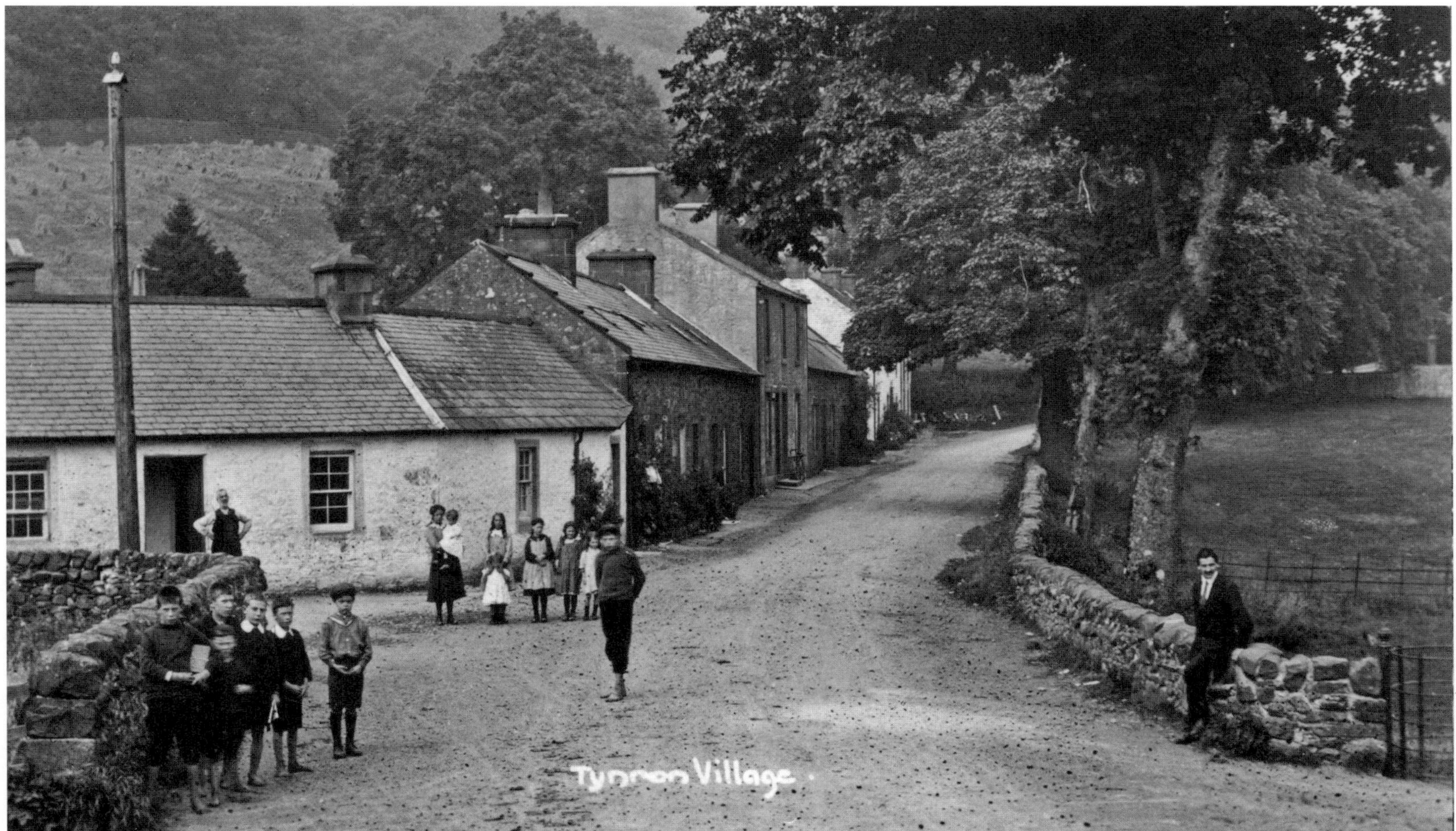

Tynron village, in the early 1900s, in the days when a passing photographer could still draw onlookers like a magnet. The low cottages date from the early-19th century, with the village post office-cum-shop situated in the taller building halfway up the lane on the left. (The eagle-eyed may spot what is possibly a postman's bicycle leaning against the wall outside!). The village was noted in the late 1880s for its Tynron Kirk Whisky, whose fame reached even to London, where it was enjoyed at the Houses of Parliament. It was blended in the churchyard and water was used from the well behind Kirkland Farmhouse. Willie Wilson, the Tynron shop keeper in the early 20th century, called 1870-1914 the Golden Years of Tynron. The village was lively with the many children. Various tradesmen flourished there: joiners, the shopkeeper, a wheelwright, a blacksmith at Parkhouse and a shoemaker. Many women were lace-makers, dressmakers, milliners, spinners and weavers.

Tynron, *c.*1916, nestling in the shadow of Craigturra and Tynron Doon. The Iron Age fort of Tynron Doon - a source of much interest to visitors - is the great local historical landmark, "unique in the picturesque landscape of mid-Nithsdale", according to old Tynronian, Wille Wilson, writing in his *Tynron in Picture, Poetry and Prose* (1927).The hill itself rises to just under 1,000 feet above sea-level.

Something of an amateur versifier, Wilson wrote of Craigturra and Tynron Doon.

To climb these hills are worth the task
The full crimson orb of the rising moon
As charcoal on canvas drawn the Craig and Doon,
In sombre, their massive forms exalt,
Round and serrate to the galaxy vault..."

The Post Office, Tynron, *c.*1913. Rural post offices have been under threat for decades and many of them have disappeared over the last thirty years or so. It was a very different story, however, in the first half of the 20th century, when most villages - even small ones like Tynron - were able to support their own full-time post office; a very useful amenity in an age when few people had cars to drive into the nearest town. Tynron's post office closed during the 1970s. I understand - from John Shaw's book *Tynron Glen* (1996) – that the figure standing on the right of the photo is that of Jimmy Laurie, who kept the village shop and post office until 1914 and made the famous Tynron Kirk Whisky.

The Endowed Public School, Tynron, *c*.1905. A fascinating account of schooling in Tynron is given in Shaw's *Tynron Glen*. Apparently, there was a school in the village as early as 1703. The Endowed School was built in 1765 and 46 pupils were recorded in attendance in 1836. The number stood at 55 in 1880 but had dropped dramatically by the end of the First World War. The Endowed School eventually closed a few months before the outbreak of the Second World War, by which time the number of children on the roll had dropped to single figures. There was also a parish school in Tynron which did not close until the late 1950s.